TIPS FOR SUCCESS™

TOP 10 TIPS FOR BUILDING STRONG FAMILY RELATIONSHIPS

KATHY FURGANG

ROSEN PUBLISHING®

NEW YORK

For Mom

Published in 2013 by The Rosen Publishing Group, Inc.
29 East 21st Street, New York, NY 10010

Library of Congress Cataloging-in-Publication Data

Furgang, Kathy.
Top 10 tips for building strong family relationships/Kathy Furgang.—1st ed.
    p. cm.—(Tips for success)
Includes bibliographical references and index.
ISBN 978-1-4488-6861-2 (library binding)
1. Families—Psychological aspects. 2. Interpersonal relations. I. Title.
HQ519.F87 2013
306.85—dc23

2011052047

Manufactured in the United States of America

CPSIA Compliance Information: Batch #S12YA: For further information, contact Rosen Publishing, New York, New York, at 1-800-237-9932.

CONTENTS

INTRODUCTION

Are you arguing with your parents again? Is your brother or sister driving you crazy? You are not alone. Millions of teens around the world experience the same family problems as you do. People often say they wish they could pick their family members. Imagine if you could choose the mother, father, sister, or brother you wanted. Of course you would pick someone with whom you could get along and who would let you do the things you want to do. You would choose brothers or sisters who were best friends. Life would be great if that were the case.

The fact is that people don't usually get to choose their family members. For the most part, we are born into or adopted by our families, and we must get along with them as best we can. Our parents teach us from the time we are born or first come into our lives. They help us grow and learn. But as children get older, they begin to want to make decisions for themselves. The

Family members must continue to work on relationships and spend quality time with each other, especially once children reach their teen years.

teen years can be especially difficult on parent-and-child rela-tionships. Teens are not children anymore, but they are not yet adults. Parents know that their children are going through stages of life that are new, confusing, and a little scary. Often the rules and expectations set by parents are meant to help teens, but they can backfire and create resentments and problems that fester and build over time.

If you are willing to put in the effort to improve family relation-ships, however, you might find the time and effort extremely well spent. An Australian study from the University of Queensland's Centre for Youth Substance Abuse Research and the Centre for Adolescent Health in Melbourne shows that strong family rela-tionships help teens steer clear of drugs and alcohol. They also help teens stay out of trouble with the authorities, such as police or school officials. For many teens, improved academic perfor-mance is also a benefit of strong family relationships.

So what is the secret to getting along with your family? There is no one secret to helping you create nurturing and sustaining family relationships. There are, however, sensible tips to help you make it through your teen years with as few problems as possible, with the strength and support of family members eas-ing your passage. If you take these to heart and work hard to put them into practice, your family members may become your greatest source of love, understanding, and strength.

TIP #1

KNOW THAT FAMILY COMES IN ALL SHAPES AND SIZES

When you say the word "family," what comes to mind? For many of us, it is a 1950s' picture of perfection, with a mom and dad, two kids, a dog, and a white picket fence around their beautiful suburban home. Why does this stereotypical image still come to so many people's minds when, in many cases, that's no longer what the American family looks like? Today's families have divorced parents, separated parents, remarried parents, grandparent caregivers, adopted children, stepchildren, stepparents, parents of different races, and parents of the same sex. When you learn to accept that families come in

Families span several generations and involve every member. Older family members set good examples and provide valuable support for younger family members.

all shapes and sizes—that there is no "typical" family—you will be more likely to feel that your family is "normal," no matter what it looks like or how it is composed.

According to the U.S. Census Bureau, only three out of ten children live in families with two parents who are in their first or only marriage. Half of American children will live with just one parent for at least part of their childhood. Nearly 33 percent of children live with a stepparent. And some children don't even live with either of their parents; 6 percent of American children live with their grandparents instead of their parents.

The fact is, nontraditional families function the same way that traditional families do. They are just as much a family as any other family you may see or know. Even children who are adopted or live in increasingly common one-parent homes must realize that a family is a family, no matter who is in charge, how big it is, and whether or not the caregivers are their birth parents.

TEENS WITH DIVORCED PARENTS

Teens of recently divorced parents may have a difficult time adjusting to a new family reality. They may wish for the days when both parents were together. They may not adjust well to living in two homes or meeting a parent's new boyfriend or girlfriend. Accepting the new reality of your family is the best way to thrive in it. It helps to realize that you are not in a family that is "messed up." Instead, you are in a very common family situation. About 40 to 50 percent of marriages end in divorce, so you are far from alone.

THE FAMILY TREE

In the modern family, making a family tree can be a challenge. Traditional family trees are based on birth parents and blood relatives, but in many families today, children may not know who their true birth parents are. One's parents may have been raised by caregivers who were not their birth parents. While a family tree may explain blood relations, it does not indicate who raised or cared for a person. One child may have been raised by just one parent and several stepparents. The tree branches of a true family should indicate not only blood relations (whom the child may have never even met), but also a child's primary caregivers and all the important stepfamily members and family friends who played crucial roles in raising and nurturing that child.

TEENS WITH STEPPARENTS

When parents remarry, children end up with more parents than they originally bargained for. Sometimes the stepparents are a welcome addition to the family, easing the stress and strain of living in a one-parent household. But other times the presence of a new stepparent may inspire confusion or conflict within the family.

Children and teens often feel overwhelmed by having a new parental figure in the household, especially one who has rule-making and rule-enforcing authority. When children feel that the stepparent does not have the right to make rules in the house, they may try to subvert his or her authority by challenging or breaking those rules. This can lead to an even more strained relationship with the child's parent, who feels caught in the middle between his or her children and the new spouse. The added pressures on the child who is being asked to accept a new step-parent can cause overall family strife that puts enormous strain on everyone.

When the family comes to a consensus about the family rules—after group discussion, debate, and agreement—and everyone understands them, then children can live more comfortably and happily within those rules.

FOSTER TEENS

According to the Administration for Children and Families, there are more than 463,000 children living in foster care in the United States. The Los Angeles County Department of Children and Family Services has indicated that close to 19

An increasing number of children and teens are being brought up in homes with same-sex parents. These families are every bit as loving, supportive, and healthy as more traditional ones.

percent of the children in foster care in California were removed from their homes because of physical abuse. The others were removed because of emotional or sexual abuse, or some other inability of the caretaker to provide for the child (because of jail time or illness, for example). While authorities try to place children with other relatives, it is not always possible to do that and children must live in a foster group home or with an assigned foster family.

While this may not be an ideal situation, foster families can be incredibly loving and supportive. They can have a huge impact on a young person's life, even if the stay is a short one. In the end, a family is loving people who surround you, nurture you, look out for you, and care for you. If you find such people through foster care, it is important to appreciate what they are doing for you and make the most of the opportunity that they are providing.

TEENS WITH SAME-SEX PARENTS

Psychiatry professors at the University of California at San Francisco and the University of Amsterdam published a study in 2010 that tested the behavior and development of children born to mothers with same-sex partners. The study found that the children performed the same as children of heterosexual parents in terms of developmental and behavioral issues.

The study also found that the children of same-sex parents performed better than children of heterosexual parents in other important areas. Confidence, self-esteem, and academic performance were higher for the children of same-sex parents. The children did experience teasing and discrimination from other children. Yet the stress the teasing caused seemed to disappear by the age of seventeen, and the children ended up being more confident than their peers. Parental involvement was cited as one of the main reasons the children were so well adjusted.

CUT YOUR PARENTS SOME SLACK

Remember the days when you were a child and you would do anything to get your parents' attention and approval? You may have pictures around the house of you as a toddler, smiling and hugging your parents. They were your best friends in the world. What ever happened to those days?

You've grown an immeasurable amount since that time, physically, intellectually, and emotionally. You are no longer that small child anymore, and your parents are no longer parents to that baby anymore. Every time you get older and hit new milestones in your childhood and youth, your parents hit new milestones as parents.

Like it or not, your family is aging and evolving. You are all growing. As part of this process, a family life that once seemed ideal and harmonious is now showing signs of strain and fractures. Don't worry—this is normal. When young children disobey their parents, they still realize that the parents are the ones in charge. As a teen, however, you begin to desire and deserve more autonomy, a greater ability and freedom to take charge of your own life. You have a natural urge to run your own life in preparation for adulthood.

THEY STILL SEE ME AS A CHILD

Just as you are probably experiencing more stress as a teen than you did as a child, your parents are also experiencing greater anxiety when raising a teen. When you were first born, diaper changes

The stress and strain of family relationships increase for both the parent and the child during the teen years as differences of opinion and misunderstandings often increase.

and feedings were the primary concern for your well-being. As the years wore on, your parents taught you more and more, but perhaps they still saw you as a child. Some parents have trouble seeing their children grow older before their eyes. It takes a lot of experience to raise a child. Just when they are beginning to feel comfortable raising a seven-year-old, the child is suddenly older and they have a whole new set of issues to deal with in raising a twelve-year-old. Now they don't worry just about the basics of your food and shelter, but also about troubling things that are partly beyond their control—your friends, dating, driving, drugs, and alcohol.

INVITE YOUR PARENTS INTO THE FRIENDSHIP CIRCLE

If you've noticed that your parents are having trouble identifying with your changing life, you may want to help them see where you are coming from—and where you hope to be heading. You may have new friends that your parents haven't met and don't know. Why not get everyone together so that your parents can meet your new friends and their parents? When you were a baby, your parents chatted with other parents about what it was like to have a baby. As the teen years approach, parents become more isolated from their children's friends and from other parents. Maintaining a circle of friends that extends to and includes parents can be very useful in promoting mutual communication, trust, and understanding. It will also give your parents their own opportunity to make new friends and have people to chat with about their parenting anxieties and strategies and the problems today's teens face.

Even when children reach their teen years, their parents may have trouble accepting the fact that "their babies" are growing up. They may feel unequipped to raise someone your age because, if you are the oldest child in the family, they have never done it before. This is why some teens notice that their parents are stricter with the oldest child and more lenient with the younger ones. Once they have had the experience of parenting a teenager, they feel more comfortable with their decisions and ease up a bit.

If you are the oldest child in your family, you may have an additional struggle to get your parents to see things your way. And if your household now has one parent instead of two, the decisions may be even more difficult for a parent to make alone. Their first instinct may be to hold you close and set strict guidelines. Understanding that your family is in new parenting territory helps the whole transition happen more smoothly. Try to recognize that your parents are anxious—even scared—as you stand on the cusp of adulthood. They are sad to see their baby separate from them. They love you deeply, and they want to see you reach adulthood in a healthy and happy state. Try to understand this and give your parents the benefit of the doubt as they try to find the best way to guide you through the teen years.

THEY DON'T UNDERSTAND ME

Not only are the situations that you come across at school—new friends, dating, peer pressure, and higher academic expectations—new to you and your family, your shifting moods are also a recent development that your parents have not had to deal with previously and are coming to terms with. Parents may try to overpower a teen's moods in hopes that they will go away. They may try too hard to cheer you up or tell you to "snap out of it."

Parents may also not understand that your interests may be changing along with your moods. You may want to be in a band with your friends instead of sticking with the scouting program. You may want to take art classes instead of going out for the soccer team

Take some time to think about how people in your family can help you if you are feeling confused, upset, or depressed.

again. Parents are only trying to help and stay involved in your life in a positive way. Above all, they want you to be happy and fulfilled and excel at what you choose to do. They may initially be threatened if you turn away from a long-term interest. But if your passion is genuine, they will soon come around and support you in it. The clearer you can express to your parents what you want and why, the greater chance you will have of getting them on your side.

TIP #3

COMMUNICATE, COMMUNICATE, COMMUNICATE

According to data from the Pew Internet Research Center, 75 percent of teens own cell phones. Thirty-three percent of those teens text more than one hundred messages each day, and some more than two hundred texts per day. So it would seem that teens are good—or at least, enthusiastic—communicators. Unfortunately, this is not the case when it comes to communicating with their parents.

COMMUNICATION IS THE KEY

Family psychologists agree that the key to good family relationships is communication. Many children stop communicating with their parents when they hit the teen years. This often happens because teens feel that their parents will not approve of their actions or understand their problems. Even teens who are facing serious trouble or experiencing overwhelming problems and who could really benefit from parental help and advice would often rather keep quiet than let their parents know. They are afraid of negative consequences or are possibly just scared or embarrassed to share information

Today's teens face difficult issues. Bullying, drugs and alcohol, dating and sex, and sexual identity are all issues that teens don't often run to their parents to discuss. But the more important the issue and the more central it is to your life, the more important it is to communicate. So why don't teens communicate more with their parents? Teens are often well aware of the "family rules," so instead of talking about issues that have violated these rules, such as trouble at school, they avoid

COMMUNICATION CAN SAVE LIVES

According to the Centers for Disease Control and Prevention, suicide is the third-leading cause of death in people age fifteen to twenty-four. It is the fourth-leading cause of death in people age ten to fourteen, and the rate of teen suicide is rising. The leading cause of suicide for teens is depression, followed by divorce of parents and violence in the home. With statistics like these, it is clear why teens need to communicate as much as possible. If you can't talk to a parent, find someone else to talk to who is able to offer wise and mature counsel.

Cutting off the lines of communication with parents can put teens at risk. Communication may not be easy, but it may help prevent larger problems from forming.

talking to the parent at all. This isolates both the parent and the child, and the problems go unsolved.

OVERCOMING RELUCTANCE AND OPENING CHANNELS OF COMMUNICATION

Many teens are afraid to talk to their parents about serious problems, and they don't think their parents will care or understand if they discuss their smaller, everyday problems. After years of growing up in the family, teens think they can predict what their parents would say anyway, and they fear getting lectured about topics they don't care to discuss. The end result of all this is closed channels of communication and a growing emotional distance between teens and their parents.

Sometimes teens try to communicate with their parents and are met with disapproval, anger, or incomprehension. The conversation does not go the way they planned or hoped. Even if you are disappointed with the conversations you have with your parent, stepparent, or caregiver, remember that they aren't perfect and they are trying to help. Even if the conversations are awkward and difficult, remember that flawed communication is far better than no communication. You are laying the groundwork for more successful conversations in the near future.

Who knows? Adults might even surprise you and be able to understand what you're going through and help you out. If they can't solve every one of your problems, they may be able to point out options, strategies, and remedies that hadn't occurred to you before. They also know you better than anyone else, even your best friends, since they've been with you for so long, possibly from birth. So they can recognize anything you are suffering that is unusual, out of character, or needs immediate attention, like depression, anxiety, or suicidal thoughts. Tragedies may be prevented or avoided if teens can communicate openly and honestly with a trusted adult.

LISTEN UP!

Communication is such an important part of good family relationships that teens need to understand that it goes both ways. Listening to your parents is just as important as parents listening to you. Teens may be quick to say, "I've heard this lecture before," or "I know, I know, you've told me this a million times." But take a minute and think about what your parents are actually saying.

The fact that you have heard their advice before and can probably recite it in your sleep doesn't make it any less important. Remember that parents have been there before. They've been teens. They've faced bullying. They've faced peer pressure. They've had boyfriend or girlfriend trouble. They've even faced problems communicating with their parents. Teens may be quick to point out the mistakes their parents have made. They may be tempted to point out that their parents' mistakes make them less qualified to give advice. But think about it. Perhaps someone who has made mistakes before and learned from them is actually well-qualified to give advice. Use a little common sense and heed sensible warnings when they are given.

CHOOSE YOUR BATTLES

Parents often remind their children to do their chores or help out around the house. Teens often tune these requests out. Yet doing things that make the house operate more smoothly and create a more pleasant physical and emotional environment, such as completing chores when asked, can go a long way toward making parents happy.

Parents sometimes get the child-rearing advice "Choose your battles"; not every issue is worth fighting over. This is good advice for teens, too. Choosing only the most important things to discuss and debate will make the battle more effective. For example, when asked to do simple chores around the house, some teens will fight their parents about it. That increases the amount of fighting in the household and puts extra pressure on family relationships.

Doing chores is a part of being an active family member. Arguing about chores can add extra pressure to already strained family relationships.

BE A FAMILY ROLE MODEL

Don't forget that younger siblings look to older siblings to learn ways to behave and act in the household. Teens have a great opportunity to help model the right kind of behavior for their younger siblings. Younger brothers and sisters will have a better chance in life if they are shown where they should be heading as they get older and how they should act as they get there. Being a good role model will also enrich family relationships and strengthen the bonds between your parents, your siblings, and yourself.

Simply doing the chores not only cuts down on the number of household arguments, but it also makes parents feel that there is a sense of order and control in the home. Believe it or not, this can make more time and room in your life for the more important discussions and "battles." It will also make parents feel that you are a mature and responsible member of the family, one who is working hard on its account. Because of this, they will be better disposed to hear and respect your opinions, perspectives, and requests.

REAP THE BENEFITS

When parents feel that you are listening to them and have respect for them, there is a much better chance that they will listen to you. Even though parents have already experienced the teen years for themselves, they can still use some help from you in understanding what teen life is like today. If they see you as an esteemed member of the household, they may be more

A relationship with a parent can become a friendship and source of support and understanding that lasts a lifetime.

willing to listen to you. You can think of this as a sort of reward for listening to your parents.

Often teens refuse to do what their parents ask as a way of showing their anger toward something their parents will not let them do. This approach often backfires because it causes a downward spiral of mutual anger, resentment, and miscommunication. The parents are less likely to listen to the teen's request because they are angry at the teen's refusal to follow family rules. On the other hand, the fewer times a parent has to point out that you are not being a helpful member of the household, the more successfully you will be able to argue a certain point that is important to you.

MAKE FRIENDS WITHIN YOUR FAMILY

If you were asked to pick your best friend in the world, would you pick your sibling? Some teens have trouble with their sibling relationships. While some are great friends, others have difficulty relating to each other. Many half siblings and stepsiblings also have difficulties with each other.

Getting along with siblings is an important part of good family relationships. Very often, siblings are the family members closest to you in age, and they are more involved in your life than cousins or more distant family members. Your siblings may go to the same school you go to and know many of the same people. Being able to get along with a sibling is important if a household is to function with a minimum of tension and conflict, and if school life is to be successful.

ONLY-CHILD SYNDROME

Years ago, many childhood development experts used to frown upon the idea of the only child. They thought that a child growing up with no siblings would not be socially well-adjusted and learn important skills like sharing, empathy, and conflict resolution. Words such as "spoiled," "bossy," and "lonely" were used to describe only children. According to Susan Newman, a social psychologist at Rutgers University, there have been no studies to confirm these claims. In fact, studies have shown that only children have some advantages that children in larger families do not have. According to the research, only children have higher test scores and higher levels of achievement and education. And only children are becoming more common as well. The number of one-child households has more than doubled in the past generation from just 10 percent to more than 20 percent. That means, one out of five families is a one-child family.

SIBLING RIVALRY

Some sibling rivalries can be intense and hurtful for a family. One of the most common reasons for sibling rivalry is jealousy. A teen may feel that his or her brother or sister has more friends, is more athletic, is better looking, or gets more attention and approval from their parents. The sibling may feel that his or her sibling has better abilities or talents or is smarter. The sibling may be more popular or have an easier time adjusting to academic and social life. Whatever the reason for the jealousy and rivalry, the tension between the two siblings may become intense.

Sibling relationships last a lifetime, so it would greatly benefit you to become friends rather than rivals.

Siblings in larger families have trouble with sibling rivalries as well. Two or more siblings may be close with each other and have a strong relationship, and another sibling may feel left out as a result. It can almost feel like a clique within the family. The family relationships among siblings may be complex, and there could be many reasons for this. The point is to remember that relationships between your siblings will most likely change. So be patient and work at the relationships. Sibling relationships last an entire lifetime. If you can build a solid friendship with your siblings, you can reap the benefits of the relationship all your life.

FRIENDS FOR LIFE

While friends may come and go throughout your lifetime, sibling relationships remain until old age. For many people, this is the only relationship that lasts so long. Children and teens do not tend to think far into their future, but it's a useful exercise to help you realize how important your siblings are. Many siblings end up having to work together as adults to take care

Siblings are siblings for life. Throughout your life, you will have to work hard to keep family friendships strong, active, and healthy.

of their parents or their affairs when their parents get too old or ill to handle things themselves. They may be faced with the task of taking care of their siblings' children in the case of an emergency or death in the family. Siblings will have an entire lifetime of memories together. If you make some effort now, you will have treasured memories to take into adulthood. And you will have the opportunity to create more good memories with your siblings at every stage of life.

10 GREAT QUESTIONS
TO ASK A FAMILY THERAPIST

1 WHAT CAN I DO IF I THINK MY PARENTS AREN'T LISTENING TO ME?

2 DO I HAVE TO COMMUNICATE WITH MY STEPPARENTS ALSO?

3 HOW MUCH SHOULD I TELL MY PARENTS ABOUT MY PERSONAL LIFE?

4 HOW CAN I MAKE MY PARENTS CHANGE THE WAY THEY TALK TO ME?

5 WHY DO OTHER FAMILIES COMMUNICATE BETTER THAN MINE?

6 WHY SHOULD I BOTHER TO TELL MY PARENTS THINGS IF THEY JUST GET ANGRY AT ME?

7 WHY DO I FIND IT EASIER TO TALK TO MY STEPPARENTS THAN MY PARENTS?

8 IS IT OK TO COMMUNICATE MORE WITH ONE PARENT THAN ANOTHER?

9 HOW CAN I LEARN TO COMMUNICATE WITH MY FAMILY BETTER?

10 WHO CAN I TALK TO WHEN I FEEL I CAN'T TALK TO MY PARENTS ABOUT SOMETHING IMPORTANT?

VALUE YOUR EXTENDED AND BLENDED FAMILY

hen teens think of their family relationships, they often don't think beyond their parents and siblings. After all, that's enough to keep any teen busy. The immediate family relationship is the one that sets the rules that teens live by. Parents and siblings are the ones who influence a teen's life the most.

But extended and blended families are also an important part of most teens' lives and interpersonal relationships. Being close to grandparents and aunts and uncles helps you get closer to your parents. Understanding where your parents came from is useful if you are trying to comprehend what makes them tick and what guides their parenting decisions. Stepfamilies are a whole new group of people that can turn out to be good friends and a helpful support network. A teen who just went through a difficult divorce may suddenly be confronted with a whole new family to vacation with, live with, or talk to. Taking an interest in the new family and learning about them can help you fit in with them.

CONNECTING WITH GRANDPARENTS

Grandparents are also a great support network. About 6 percent of American families live with a grandparent, and many others may see their grandparents frequently. However, many teens grow distant from their grandparents. They often visit with and talk to them less as they grow older. They may remember them

Grandparents and other extended family members help make you who you are. You can learn a lot about your family, your parents, and yourself through these relationships.

more as the grandparents they knew as children but not ever get to know them as people.

Just as parent-and-child relationships go through changes in the teen years, grandparent-and-grandchild relationships must also evolve and change in order to flourish. Learning about your grandparents' lives may be much more fascinating than you think. They may have lived through many of the historic events you are learning about in school, such as wars, protests, immigrations, the civil rights movement, or other events that may surprise you. Reaching out to grandparents is a great way to get to know the family that you are part of and discover that your family history is richer than you thought it was.

EXTENDING THE BOUNDARIES OF THE EXTENDED FAMILY

Remember that family is what we make it. When you think of your extended family, the operative word is "extended." Godparents and extremely close family friends can sometimes be considered family. Sometimes when families live far away from their blood relatives, close family friends are the best support group. These people may know you better than your extended family and be able to help you with problems. While the term "family" often refers to a group of people related by blood or marriage, it also refers to a close-knit group of people. Consider your extended family to be people whom you feel close to and would be proud to call "family."

Learning about your extended family also helps you learn about your culture, which is part of your history and who you are. If teens learn about their family's ethnic or religious history, they can develop a greater sense of family identity and a stronger sense of their own place within it.

A BUILT-IN SUPPORT NETWORK

Even after making an effort to communicate with their immediate family or seek help from them, teens may not get all of the emotional support they need. They may need to go to others for help. While you may consider friends, counselors, teachers, or other adult mentors, extended family is also a great resource for emotional support that you may need. What better person with whom to discuss a problem relating to your dad than his brother or sister who grew up with him and knows him inside and out? Who better to talk with about a problem at school than your cousins who understand the pressures you face at your age? Who better to help you with math subjects than a stepgrandparent who was an engineer? Even the most ordinary family can be filled with talented, caring, and patient people who can help you through problems.

TIP #7

ACCEPT IMPERFECTIONS, AND DON'T GIVE UP ON THE FAMILY

Teens spend a lot of time with friends, so they get a lot of exposure to the way that other families operate. They often end up wishing that their own family operated like others. One of the most common arguments that teens make is, "Well, Anna's parents let her do it." You might be able to guess what the parents would say in response to this comment. It would likely be something like, "Well, we're not Anna's parents!"

Each family is unique, and each family makes its own decisions for its own reasons. This sometimes makes teens envious of other families and curious about what it might be like to live in their households. Accepting your own family, with all of its seeming flaws, is one of the most important tips for developing and maintaining good family relationships. Instead of hating or resenting your family because of its imperfections, learn to love your family despite its imperfections.

What may work for one family may not work for another. The dynamics of families are different from one to another because of the organization of parents and children in the household. The personalities and circumstances of each family are different as well. If you think that your family should be like Anna's family, you may not be seeing the situation in a realistic way. You also may not be seeing the whole picture: Anna may have issues that she would desperately like to change and may think of your family as the way she wishes her own family could be.

GETTING HELP

Family therapists can often help families as well as individuals work through issues and problems. If family members are reluctant to try group therapy, the teen should seek it for himself or herself to make sure he or she is getting the help needed. Going to a school counselor can help. Starting with a school counselor is a good idea. The counselor can help you decide who else you should speak to, such as a professional therapist or, in cases in which the home is a place of danger, someone from law enforcement. The school counselor may also be able to persuade the family to give group therapy a try. You should never feel that you must deal with difficult issues all by yourself.

EVERY FAMILY IS IMPERFECT

Accept the fact that your family has imperfections. Sometimes these imperfections may be huge. They may seem insurmountable. Family members may have physical or mental illnesses that others may not understand. There may be money problems or unemployment in a family. Families may be forced to relocate frequently because of military or work obligations. There may be family members in jail or treatment and rehab facilities for drug or alcohol problems. Siblings may be failing out of school or be involved with gangs or drugs. Physical, emotional, or sexual abuse may be present in a family.

A family may be terribly flawed, but it shouldn't be given up on. First and foremost, do what you must to protect yourself and make yourself safe. If you are in a dangerous or damaging situation within the family, get outside help and remove yourself from the danger. Then seek help for family problems to start the healing. Get individual therapy or counseling, as well as family therapy. If the family can survive its troubles intact, it will emerge stronger and better able to weather future storms.

ACCEPTANCE AND KINDNESS WITHIN THE FAMILY

Even if your family isn't experiencing dramatic problems like these, no family is perfect. You may find that searching for perfection will not make your family become what you think you want it to be; it will only emphasize your problems all the more. Of course, it is very important to work out problems, but accepting your family members for who they are is a good way to foster closer family relationships. After all, you expect them to accept you for who you are, so returning the favor and embracing them, warts and all, is the right thing to do.

Sometimes teens and other family members let the insults fly. While it is a good idea to be honest with your family, being deliberately hurtful does not do anyone any good. For example, children from divorced families may go back and forth from one household to another and develop a favorite home or parent to be with. Family relationships may become worse if the teen is vocal or spiteful about which family he or she prefers. Remember that one parent's feelings may be hurt if a teen vindictively declares that he or she enjoys being with another parent more. Remember that the issue is likely to be sensitive to your parents, so using the situation to gain some ground in family feuds may make it worse.

LOOK OUT FOR EACH OTHER

While some teens may feel that their families do not support them, other teens feel an opposite pressure from their families. Some teens feel embarrassed when their parents try to get too involved in their lives. Sometimes a parent may get involved in school events or complain to the school about small problems that the teen may be having or grades that he or she may have received. This can tend to make teens feel less independent and more like children. However, the benefits far outweigh the problems when families stick together.

STRONGER TOGETHER

The teen years are hard to navigate for anyone, and sticking together as a family is an important way to get through these difficult years. Teens may find themselves swamped by numerous problems, so it makes sense to accept help when it is offered.

Getting a parent involved in your problems can have its benefits. Your parent may have unexpected insights, ideas, or solutions that can help.

When a teen is bullied, for example, he or she may not want to get a parent involved because of embarrassment or fear of what the parent might do. But the problem may not be solvable without outside help. Confiding in family and accepting the help of parents or even older siblings can help relieve pressure and stress on family relationships. In addition to solving the problem, family bonds may be strengthened in the process.

Teens who want their families "out of their lives" may be overlooking the benefits of having adults who are on their side and want to help. This includes when families get involved in teens' personal friendships and relationships. When a parent sees that a child is involved with something that might be illegal or detrimental to his or her health, safety, or positive growth, the

A FAMILY IS A TEAM

It may help to think of your family as a team of sorts. Just as athletic team members "have each other's backs," you and your family members support each other whenever you can. Remember that when a team member needs help, others move into position and support the member in need.

parent's job is to get involved. That's just expected of any loving family. A supportive family tries its best to keep all of its members on the right path.

PUTTING THE SHOE ON THE OTHER FOOT

The road to a supportive family runs both ways. Teens should think about the importance of looking out for other family members just as much as family members may look out for them. This includes sticking up for siblings when they encounter problems in the neighborhood or at school with bullies or even friends who don't necessarily have their best interests at heart.

Parents need your support as well. Showing your support for your parents' personal endeavors is an important way to build a bond between you and your parents. Remember that adults try to improve their lives just like anybody else. Parents may try to give up smoking, get in shape, or go back to school. When a child supports their efforts, it shows that the family unit is strong. It shows that you care about your parents' well-being, health, and happiness.

GO WITH THE FLOW

When parents feel the need to punish their children, such as through grounding or a suspension of privileges, some teens let their anger get the best of them. They may feel they have been treated unfairly, so they may purposely try to make things difficult for their parents. This may come in the form of talking back, refusing to help out at home, or even blatantly defying their parents' wishes to "show them who's boss."

Unfortunately, these tactics nearly always backfire, putting the teenager in a worse situation than before. Soon the situation and the family relationship spiral out of control, making the original complaint no longer the biggest or only problem.

GO ALONG TO GET ALONG

Knowing which battles are worth fighting can keep teens from damaging already fragile relationships with parents or

You may face difficult situations in your family life, but communication—even when it's animated and passionate—should help you get through even the toughest spots. And your family relationships will be the stronger for it.

caregivers. Sometimes teens who have trouble accepting a stepparent or a parent's new girlfriend or boyfriend will go out of their way to damage the relationship or make things harder for everyone involved. Although there are definitely strong feelings involved in broken homes, trying to smooth things over and practicing a "go along to get along" philosophy are much better, more productive approaches than fruitless defiance or disobedience.

When you go with the flow, you can prevent major problems in the relationship from developing or worsening. You can avoid putting any additional wedges between you and your family members. That means making compromises and trying to resolve your conflicts fairly and calmly. Escalating a

TAKE PART IN YOUR FAMILY

Teens who are having trouble with their families tend to distance themselves and not take part in family outings or other events during which the family could be blowing off steam and bonding. This causes a deeper problem because when the teens are absent or sullen, parents bond with younger siblings. Be there in your family. Be a member, and take your place in the family structure. Just being present is half the battle. You may be surprised at how family dynamics shift and loosen up when you are all out of the house and in a more relaxed setting.

disagreement into a shouting match almost always has disappointing and unproductive results. On the other hand, working through a problem can only make the relationship stronger and increase a sense of mutual trust, respect, kindness, compassion, support, and generosity.

SHEDDING A BAD REPUTATION

Family members tend to get reputations. A sibling may be branded as "the smart one" or "the pretty one." Another child may be known as "the difficult one." When a teen gets a reputation based on his or her behavior, it becomes difficult to overcome it. Parents may expect a fight from you over every issue. That may actually undermine the strength of your argument and their willingness to listen to and consider it.

Showing a little willingness to compromise goes a long way in a family that has trouble functioning. Even though you may

Be an active member of your family. Get involved in what is going on in the family and be willing to compromise.

disagree with your parents' decision to ground you for coming home from the movies later than you said you would, think about the consequences of fighting. The issue may escalate, you may lose more privileges, and then you may really miss out on something you care about doing.

IF AT FIRST YOU DON'T SUCCEED, TRY, TRY AGAIN!

Family relationships must be worked on constantly, whether it's the parents' relationship with each other (including ex-spouses and stepparents), the parents' relationship with the child, or the siblings' relationship with each other. Major and/or repeated arguments with loved ones can make teens want to give up. They may reject their parents' efforts in the future or turn their backs on their attempts to fix the problem. But this will not help in the long run. Keep trying to solve problems and heal relationships. Try as many times as needed. Each time, try a fresh approach or make a new effort to see the other person's point of view.

Remember that family relationships are forever, and the work that must be done to maintain and grow the relationships will last a lifetime. Each milestone in a family's life is a new chance to make improvements. Even families that get along must make efforts to maintain their good relationships with each other. Family relationships do not get fixed, or settled, for any amount of time. They are constantly evolving, and new challenges are always arriving even as old problems subside.

People's roles in their families continue to change and evolve throughout their lives. Working on strong family relationships does not end after the teen years. Family members need each other forever.

And older problems that you thought had been resolved may reoccur if families are not vigilant about always working hard on their relationships.

CHANGE AND STABILITY

Families are all about change and flux. In the case of divorced families, new marriages may occur between parents and step-parents. These second marriages may also end eventually, and a parent may remarry again. As teens become older, they, too, can become parents with a whole new set of family issues and relatives to deal with. Grandchildren change the dynamic of

Enjoy your family members and have fun spending time with them. Even the most difficult relationships can be improved and become a source of great love and joy as the years pass.

a family, and so do new romances for teens or young adults. Health care issues pop up in families as family members age. As parents age, the roles of children and parents change yet again. Children take on more responsibility than they had when they were younger, and the parents become more dependent.

Yet healthy families provide stability and security amid all this inevitable change and flux. The enduring benefits of family continue throughout a lifetime. Seeing a family grow and gain new members through marriage and birth can inject new life and fresh perspectives into the group.

REMEMBER THE GOOD TIMES

When teens feel like giving up on their family relationships, it may help to think back to the good times that your family has had together. When anger gets in the way, it is sometimes hard to remember the good times and what family means to us. Thinking back to your fun times as a child can help you appreciate your family and renew your commitment to do your best to make things work.

It may be difficult for a teenager to see life as such a long and enduring journey. This is often part of the reason teens feel angry and impatient about their lives. But at any age, it is worth the effort to try to heal emotional wounds with family members. A sibling, parent, stepparent, foster parent, or any extended family member can add a richness to your life and give you a sense of belonging. These relationships are lifelong experiences that can help us grow and become better people. They can even help teens better understand the importance of family so that when they are beginning to have their own families, they will be better prepared for all the ups and downs, joys and sorrows. And they will have a better idea about what to do and what not to do with their own children. Striving for healthy and solid family relationships is a lifelong struggle that is well worth the time and effort that people put into it.

MYTH: CHILDREN FROM DIVORCED FAMILIES ARE BOUND TO GET DIVORCES WHEN THEY GROW UP AND GET MARRIED.

FACT: THE MARITAL HISTORY OF ONE'S PARENTS DOES NOT AFFECT THE SUCCESS OR FAILURE OF A CHILD'S MARRIAGE. WHILE PARENTS DO PROVIDE THEIR CHILDREN WITH MODELS OF WHAT IT IS LIKE TO BE IN A MARRIAGE, THIS DOES NOT MEAN THAT A FAILED MARRIAGE IS BOUND TO BE MODELED BY THE CHILDREN OF DIVORCE.

MYTH: STEPPARENTS CANNOT LOVE STEPCHILDREN AS IF THEY ARE THEIR OWN.

FACT: EVERY FAMILY IS DIFFERENT, INCLUDING THE RELATIONSHIPS BETWEEN STEPPARENTS AND THE CHILDREN OF THEIR SPOUSES. MANY STEPPARENTS DO INDEED LOVE THEIR STEPCHILDREN AS THEIR OWN, WHETHER OR NOT THEY ALSO HAVE THEIR OWN BIOLOGICAL CHILDREN.

MYTH: PEOPLE CAN'T CHANGE, SO IT IS USELESS TO EVEN TRY.

FACT: PEOPLE CAN DEFINITELY CHANGE. PARENTHOOD ITSELF CHANGES PEOPLE, AND COUNTLESS OTHER LIFE EXPERIENCES DO AS WELL, FROM ADDICTION RECOVERY TO FORGIVING LOVED ONES. IT IS WORTH YOUR TIME AND EFFORT TO TRY TO BE THE PERSON YOU WANT TO BE. IF YOU CAN CHANGE FOR THE BETTER, SO CAN YOUR FAMILY MEMBERS AND YOUR RELATIONSHIPS WITH THEM.

ACCEPTANCE The willingness to tolerate something difficult or unpleasant and move forward.

ADOPTION The process whereby a person assumes the parenting for another and, in so doing, permanently transfers all rights and responsibilities from the original parent or parents.

COMPROMISE An agreement or settlement reached by both parties in a dispute, in which both parties usually give up something desired in order to meet in the middle.

CULTURE The customs of a particular nation, society, ethnic or religious group, or members of a group.

EXTENDED FAMILY People who are outside the immediate family unit, such as grandparents, uncles, aunts, cousins, nephews, nieces, and in-laws.

FAMILY COUNSELOR A person who gives guidance in matters dealing with the family and helps its members communicate and strengthen their relationships with each other.

FOSTER CHILD A child brought up in a private home by a state-certified caregiver who is not a parent or relative.

PSYCHOTHERAPY Any form of therapeutic interaction or treatment contracted between a trained professional and a client or patient, family, couple, or group. The problems addressed are psychological in nature. Psychotherapy aims to increase the individual's sense of his or her own well-being. Psychotherapists employ a range of techniques based on relationship building, dialogue, communication, and behavior change that are designed to improve the mental health of a client or patient, or to improve group relationships (such as in a family).

SIBLING A brother or sister.

SIBLING RIVALRY The competition between siblings in a family, often for parental attention or approval.

STEPFAMILY An extended family formed through the remarriage of divorced or widowed parents.

TRADITION The customs or beliefs that pass from one generation to the next.

Action Alliance for Children (AAC)
1201 Martin Luther King Jr. Way
Oakland, CA, 94612
(510) 444-7136
Web site: http://www.4children.org
The AAC works to inform, educate, connect, and inspire
people who work with and on behalf of children.

Administration for Children and Families (ACF)
370 L'Enfant Promenade SW
Washington, DC 20447
Web site: http://www.acf.hhs.gov
The ACF is a division of the Department of Health and
Human Services. It is in charge of federal programs
that support families and promote healthy child
development.

American Academy of Child and Adolescent Psychiatry
(AACAP)
3615 Wisconsin Avenue NW
Washington, DC 20016-3007
(202) 966-7300
Web site: http://www.aacap.org
The AACAP is the leading national professional medical
association dedicated to treating and improving the
quality of life for children, adolescents, and families
affected by mental, emotional, behavioral, and
developmental disorders.

American Association for Marriage and Family Therapy
   (AAMFT)
112 South Alfred Street
Alexandria, VA 22314
(703) 838-9808
Web site: http://www.aamft.org
The AAMFT is a professional association for the field
   of marriage and family therapy. It represents the
   professional interests of more than twenty-four
   thousand marriage and family therapists throughout
   the United States, Canada, and abroad.

Children's Rights
330 Seventh Avenue, 4th Floor
New York, NY 10001
Web site: http://www.childrensrights.org
Children's Rights is a national advocacy group working
   to guarantee every child's right to grow up in a safe,
   stable, permanent home.

Child Welfare League of America (CWLA)
1726 M Street NW, Suite 500
Washington, DC 20036
(202) 833-1638
Web site: http://www.cwla.org
The CWLA is a powerful coalition of hundreds of private and public agencies serving children and
   families since 1920.

International Bureau for Children's Rights (IBCR)
2715 Chemin de la Côte-Sainte-Catherine
Montréal, QC H3T 1B6
Canada
(514) 932-7656
Web site: http://www.ibcr.org
The IBCR is an international nongovernmental organization based in Montreal, Canada. The IBCR's mission is to contribute to the promotion and respect of the Convention on the Rights of the Child adopted by the United Nations in 1989 and now ratified by 192 countries.

Kids' Turn
55 New Montgomery, Suite 500
San Francisco, CA 94105
(415) 777-9977
Web site: http://kidsturn.org
Kids' Turn is a nonprofit organization that aids families going through parental separation. It helps children understand and cope with the loss, anger, and fear that often accompany separation or divorce. It also awakens parents to the need to support their children during this crisis so that at-risk behavior by children is averted.

National Domestic Violence Hotline
P.O. Box 161810

Austin, TX 78716
(800) 799-SAFE (799-7233)
Web site: http://www.thehotline.org
The National Domestic Violence Hotline provides help
    24 hours a day, 7 days a week in more than 170
    languages for people needing help with domestic
    violence issues.

Rainbows Canada
80 Bradford Street, Suite 545
Barrie, ON L4N 6S7
Canada
(877) 403-2733
Web site: http://www.rainbows.ca
Rainbows Canada is an international, nonprofit organi-
    zation that fosters emotional healing among children
    suffering from a life-altering crisis. These crises can
    include separation, divorce, death, incarceration,
    and foster care.

U.S. Department of Health and Human Services (HHS)
200 Independence Avenue SW
Washington, DC 20201
(877) 696-6775
Web site: http://www.hhs.gov
The HHS is a government agency designed to protect
    the health and well-being of Americans, including
    that of the American family.

WEB SITES

Due to the changing nature of Internet links, Rosen Publishing has developed an online list of Web sites related to the subject of this book. This site is updated regularly. Please use this link to access the list:

http://www.rosenlinks.com/top10/fam

FOR FURTHER READING

Canfield, Jack, and Mark Victor Hansen. *Chicken Soup for the Soul: Teens Talk Relationships: Stories About Family, Friends, and Love*. New York, NY: Chicken Soup for the Soul, 2008.

Cohn, Lisa, and Debbie Glasser. *The Step-Tween Survival Guide: How to Deal with Life in a Stepfamily*. Minneapolis, MN: Free Spirit Publishing, 2008.

Deal, Ron L. *The Smart Step-Family: Seven Steps to a Healthy Family*. Ada, MI: Bethany House, 2006.

Fox, Annie. *What's Up with My Family?* Minneapolis, MN: Free Spirit Publishing, 2010.

Johnson, Leona. *Strengthening Family and Self*. Tinley Park, IL: Goodheart-Willcox, 2010.

Johnston, Kurt, and Mark Oestreicher. *My Family*. El Cajon, CA: Zondervan/Youth Specialties, 2007.

Lynch, Amy. *A Smart Girl's Guide to Understanding Her Family*. Middleton, WI: American Girl, 2009.

Michaels, Vanessa Lynn, and Jeremy Harrow. *Frequently Asked Questions About Family Violence*. New York, NY: Rosen Publishing, 2010.

Orr, Tamra. *Home and Family Relationships* (Teens: Being Gay, Lesbian, Bisexual, or Transgender). New York, NY: Rosen Publishing, 2010.

Schab, Lisa M. *The Divorce Workbook for Teens: Activities to Help You Move Beyond the Breakup*. Oakland, CA: Instant Help Books, 2008.

Sindell, Max. *The Bright Side: Surviving Your Parents' Divorce*. Deerfield Beach, FL: Health Communications, 2007.

Smith, Krista. *The Big D: Divorce Thru the Eyes of a Teen: Student Workbook*. Scottsdale, AZ: AMFM Press, 2010.

Trueit, Trudi Strain. *Surviving Divorce: Teens Talk About What Hurts and What Helps*. New York, NY: Franklin Watts, 2007.

Barkley, Russell A., and Arthur L. Robin. *Your Defiant Teen: 10 Steps to Resolve Conflict and Rebuild Your Relationship*. New York, NY: Guilford Press, 2008.

Center for Young Women's Health. "Healthy Relationships." Retrieved October 2011 (http://www.youngwomenshealth.org/healthy_relat.html).

Children Uniting Nations. "Foster Care Statistics." Retrieved October 2011 (http://www.childrenuniting nations.org/who-we-are/foster-care-statistics).

Communication Studies. "Teen Cell Phone Statistics." April 18, 2011. Retrieved October 2011 (http://www.communicationstudies.com/teen-cell-phone-statistics-infographic).

DuPont, Sandra. "Improve Your Family's Relationships." Teen Therapist. Retrieved October 2011 (http://santamonicateentherapist.com/improving-your-family-relationships).

Feinstein, Sheryl. *Inside the Teenage Brain: Parenting a Work in Progress*. Lanham, MD: R&L Education, 2009.

Konner, Melvin. *The Evolution of Childhood: Relationships, Emotion, Mind*. Cambridge, MA: Belknap Press, 2011.

Maxym, Carol. "Inside the Teenage Brain: Talking with Your Teen." PBS.org, 2001. Retrieved October 2011 (http://www.pbs.org/wgbh/pages/frontline/shows/teenbrain/etc/worksheet.html).

Medical Xpress. "Family Relationships May Protect Early Teens from Alcohol Use." June 7, 2011. Retrieved October 2011 (http://medicalxpress.com/news/2011-06-family-relationships-early-teens-alcohol.html).

Park, Alice. "Study: Children of Lesbians May Do Better Than Their Peers." *Time*, June 7, 2010. Retrieved October 2011 (http://www.time.com/time/health/article/0,8599,1994480,00.html).

Rimm, Sylvia. "The Changing Family." Retrieved October 2011 (http://www.sylviarimm.com/article_changfam.html).

The Situationist. "Only-Child Syndrome or Advantage?" August 19, 2007. Retrieved October 2011 (http://thesituationist.wordpress.com/2007/08/19/only-child-syndrome-or-adavantage).

Smetana, Judith G. *Adolescents, Families, and Social Development: How Teens Construct Their Worlds.* New York, NY: Wiley-Blackwell, 2010.

Teen Suicide Statistics. "Teen Suicide Overview." Retrieved October 2011 (http://www.teensuicidestatistics.com).

Wallerstein, Judith S., and Sandra Blakeslee. *What About the Kids?: Raising Your Children Before, During, and After Divorce.* New York, NY: Hyperion, 2003.

INDEX

ABOUT THE AUTHOR

Kathy Furgang has written numerous books for young readers. She has a degree in psychology and has written on topics such as teen health and wellness. She lives in upstate New York with her husband and two young sons.

PHOTO CREDITS

Cover © istockphoto.com/MichaelDeLeon; p. 5 Jupiter Images/Photos.com/Getty Images/Thinkstock; p. 8 Jack Hollingsworth/Digital Vision/Thinkstock; p. 11 © istockphoto.com/elkor; p. 14 Comstock/Thinkstock; p. 17 Shutterstock/OtnaYdur; pp. 20, 45 Jupiter Images/Creatas/Thinkstock; p. 23 © istockphoto.com/Pixel_Pig; p. 25 Shutterstock/CREATISTA; p. 28 Hemera/Thinkstock; p. 29 Shutterstock/Kenneth Sponsler; p. 32 Todd Wamock/Lifesize/Thinkstock; p. 40 Ryan McVay/PhotoDisc/Thinkstock; p. 43 Buccina Studios/Photodisc/Thinkstock;p. 47 Stockbyte/Thinkstock; p. 48 Maria Teijeiro/Digital Vision/Thinkstock; back cover, interior graphic Shutterstock/phyZick.

Designer: Nicole Russo; Photo Researcher: Marty Levick